TRUCKS

OFF-ROAD VEHICLES

GARY SPROTT

BEFORE AND DURING READING ACTIVITIES

Before Reading: *Building Background Knowledge and Vocabulary*
Building background knowledge can help children process new information and build upon what they already know. Before reading a book, it is important to tap into what children already know about the topic. This will help them develop their vocabulary and increase their reading comprehension.

Questions and Activities to Build Background Knowledge:
1. Look at the front cover of the book and read the title. What do you think this book will be about?
2. What do you already know about this topic?
3. Take a book walk and skim the pages. Look at the table of contents, photographs, captions, and bold words. Did these text features give you any information or predictions about what you will read in this book?

Vocabulary: *Vocabulary Is Key to Reading Comprehension*
Use the following directions to prompt a conversation about each word.
- Read the vocabulary words.
- What comes to mind when you see each word?
- What do you think each word means?

Vocabulary Words:
- *capacity*
- *commercial*
- *convoy*
- *horsepower*
- *terrain*
- *versatile*

During Reading: *Reading for Meaning and Understanding*
To achieve deep comprehension of a book, children are encouraged to use close reading strategies. During reading, it is important to have children stop and make connections. These connections result in deeper analysis and understanding of a book.

Close Reading a Text
During reading, have children stop and talk about the following:
- Any confusing parts
- Any unknown words
- Text to text, text to self, text to world connections
- The main idea in each chapter or heading

Encourage children to use context clues to determine the meaning of any unknown words. These strategies will help children learn to analyze the text more thoroughly as they read.

When you are finished reading this book, turn to the next-to-last page for **After Reading Questions** and an **Activity**.

TABLE OF
CONTENTS

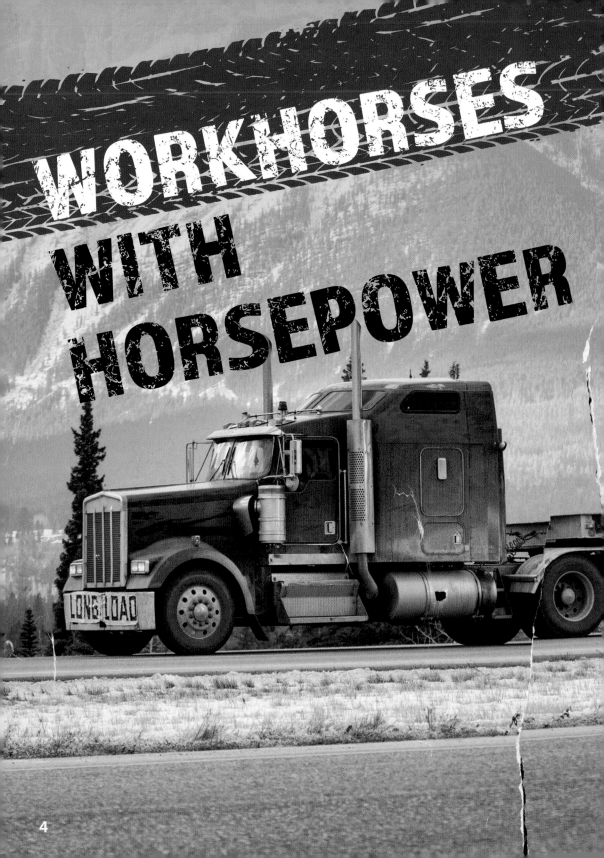

WORKHORSES
WITH
HORSEPOWER

Tough and trusty! Trucks have been hauling loads for more than 120 years. On construction sites, highways, ranches, farms, loading docks, and logging roads, a truck is a tried-and-true friend.

Keep On Truckin'

Four wheels, 6 wheels, 10 wheels, and 18 wheels! Light duty, heavy duty, super duty, and big rigs! From pickups to semis, there's a truck for every job.

Carrying and towing heavy cargo calls for lots of muscle. Luckily, trucks have plenty of **horsepower** under the hood. Horsepower tells how much raw power and capacity for work a vehicle has. It's based on how much work a big horse can do!

horsepower (HORS-pou-ur): a unit for measuring the power of an engine

A semi truck can churn out more than 670 horsepower.

The German company Daimler-Motoren-Gesellschaft built the world's first truck in 1896. This motorized **commercial** vehicle looked like a horse-drawn cart—without the horse! It had a gas-powered engine and wooden wheels wrapped in iron.

commercial (kuh-MUR-shuhl): for sale, or having to do with buying and selling

No Horsing Around!
Daimler's four-horsepower truck was not a big hit. Nobody in Germany wanted to buy one. Strange, since this little pony didn't need to be fed hay or have someone pick up poop behind it!

In the 21st century, many of the world's biggest automobile companies manufacture trucks. Ford, Chevrolet, Nissan, GMC, Toyota, and Dodge are popular brands. A pickup truck is the favorite set of wheels for lots of drivers—even those who haul nothing more than groceries!

Terrific Trio

The three best-selling vehicles in the United States in 2018 were trucks. More than two million Ford F-Series, Chevy Silverados, and Dodge Rams were sold.

Pickups are marvels of might. The six-wheel Silverado 3500HD has enough power to tow loads as heavy as a couple of elephants! You could call it a pickup *trunk*!

All Work and All Play

Just because you're heading off-road doesn't mean you can't ride in style! The Ford F-150 Lariat comes with leather-trimmed seats, voice-activated and touchscreen technology, a rear-view camera, and satellite radio. "Thanks, but I'll just wait in the truck!"

LAND OF BIG RIGS

When the task calls for supersized **capacity**, it's time to call in a big rig! These giant trucks often pull a semitrailer, or semi, filled with goods of all kinds. They can haul giant boats and even houses!

capacity (kuh-PAS-i-tee): the amount that something can hold

OVERSIZE LOAD

Logging trucks must handle the roughest **terrain**. These heavy-duty haulers climb narrow, winding forest roads to collect timber. Some of the trucks have giant grapples, or grabbers, to pick up trees that have been chopped down.

terrain (tuh-RAYN): ground or land

The Caterpillar 797F mining truck is so massive that the driver has to climb a ladder to get to the steering wheel! It can carry loads of coal, copper, or dirt weighing as much as 150 Ford pickup trucks.

Fill 'Er Up

Don't get stuck behind a Caterpillar 797F at the gas station. This thirsty beast's gas tank can hold 1,000 gallons (3,785 liters).

MONSTERS AND DRAGSTERS

Stone Crusher. Devastator. Barbarian. Raminator! It sounds like a scary lineup of comic book villains. But these mutants are big-wheeled trucks—monster trucks! And they're revved up and ready to race.

Getting into a Jam!
Monster trucks compete in Monster Jam events around the world. Bone-shaking jumps, freaky flips, and wacky wheelies are all part of the fuel-injected fun.

Strength, speed, and stability make trucks **versatile** vehicles. Their bodies are high off the ground, so they can climb over obstacles. Their shock-absorbing suspension systems can handle the bumpiest surfaces.

versatile (VUR-suh-tuhl): able to function or be used in many different ways

Ever feel like taking a mud bath? Yup, we knew it. Well, you'd probably like mud bogging. It's a pretty simple sport. Drive a truck through deep ditches of mud. If you get stuck, you're out!

A Little Bit Higher

Even trucks need a little boost to—squelch!—get through a mud pit. Drivers raise, or jack up, their trucks with extra-large tires for mud bogging races.

Ready for some turbocharged drag racing? In this popular sport, trucks of all types zoom down a short, straight track. Blink and you might miss these dragsters cross the finish line!

Big Rig Hot Rods

Did we say trucks of all types? Yes, even semis burn rubber in drag racing contests. Now that's some high-speed hauling!

In Lancaster County, Pennsylvania, a **convoy** of trucks comes together each year for a good cause. The Make-a-Wish Foundation sponsors the event. Truckers give rides to children with life-threatening illnesses.

convoy (KAHN-voi): a group of vehicles that travel together for convenience or safety

Memory Game

Look at the pictures. What do you remember re
on the pages where each image appeared?

Index

After Reading Questions

1. When was the world's first truck built?
2. Which truck holds 1,000 gallons of gas?
3. What are Stone Crusher and Raminator?
4. What does horsepower measure?
5. What kind of roads do logging trucks drive on?

Activity

Monster truck racing is a popular sport. Draw and design your own monster truck. What would it look like and what equipment would it have? What would you call it?

About the Author

Gary Sprott is a writer in Tampa, Florida. He has written books about ancient cultures, animals, plants, and automobiles. Gary hopes someday he can ride in a Ford F-150 Lariat!

www.rourkeeducationalmedia.com

PHOTO CREDITS: Cover, page 1, 11: ©Ford Motor Company; pages 4-5, 30: ©Stefonlinton; page 7: ©Toyota; pages 8-9: ©Martin Durrschnabel; pages 13, 30: ©Chevy; pages 15, 30: ©vitpho; page 17, 30: ©Darin Burt; pages 18-19: ©erlucho; page 21: ©Barry Salmons; pages 22-23: ©Nigel Jarvis; page 25: ©nikitsin.smugmug.com; pages 26-27, 30: ©Peter Long, pages 29, 30: ©Delmas Lehman

Edited by: Kim Thompson
Cover and interior design by: Rhea Magaro-Wallace

Library of Congress PCN Data

Trucks / Gary Sprott
(Off-Road Vehicles)
  ISBN 978-1-73161-453-7 (hard cover)
  ISBN 978-1-73161-254-0 (soft cover)
  ISBN 978-1-73161-558-9 (e-Book)
  ISBN 978-1-73161-663-0 (ePub)
Library of Congress Control Number: 2019932310

Rourke Educational Media
Printed in the United States of America,
North Mankato, Minnesota